Early Irish Gospel Books

in the Library of Trinity College Dublin

Susan Bioletti
& Rachel Moss

Trinity College Dublin
Coláiste na Tríonóide, Baile Átha Cliath
The University of Dublin

Early Irish Gospel Books
in the Library of Trinity College Dublin
Susan Bioletti and Rachel Moss

This book was produced to celebrate the research, conservation and digitising of four of Trinity College Library's early Irish manuscripts.

The members of the early Irish manuscripts project team are sincerely thanked for all their efforts: Marco di Bella, Marta Bustillo, Brenda Cullen, John Gillis, Tim Keefe, Jane Maxwell, Bernard Meehan, Eileen Punch, Allyson Smith, Colleen Thomas, Gillian Whelan and Catherine Yvard.

Conservation of *Codex Usserianus Primus*, the *Garland of Howth*, the *Book of Dimma* and the *Book of Mulling* has been made possible thanks to the Bank of America Merrill Lynch Art Conservation Project.

Contents

Librarian's Preface

Amongst the great holdings of our Library are many unique records that attest to human endeavour and enquiry, including a small collection of the very earliest Irish gospel books. With just a handful of   complete or partial copies of these surviving world-wide, our collection of seven books includes the masterpiece, the *Book of Kells*.

 The artistry of these manuscripts provides evidence of the technical skills and creative expression that flourished in Ireland in the early medieval period. It is the unknown as much as the known that intrigues, challenges, and captivates us.

How they were made, the pigments that were used, their function and influence, and the communities that produced or used the gospels remains to be fully understood. Our manuscripts are still revealing the evidence of their histories and will continue to provide us with a wealth of information through decades to come. In these pages we share the beauty of these magnificent works, and the secrets they have revealed.

Helen Shenton,
Librarian and College Archivist

Early Irish gospel books in Trinity College Dublin

In 1007, following its theft from the church at Kells, a contemporary chronicler described the 'Great Gospel Book of Colum Cille', now better known as the *Book of Kells,* as the most precious object of the Western World. The Irish commentator might well be accused of patriotic bias, but during the early medieval period, illuminated manuscript copies of the four gospels produced for the Irish or 'Insular' Church were much admired internationally and were owned and copied by monasteries across Europe.

Today, relatively few of these precious remnants of early Christianity survive. However, the Library of Trinity College Dublin is privileged to own no fewer than seven whole or partial copies of Irish gospel books from the period, the largest collection anywhere in the world. These are the *Codex Usserianus Primus* (MS 55), the *Book of Durrow* (MS 57), the *Book of Armagh* (MS 52), the *Book of Dimma* (MS 59), the *Book of Mulling* (MS 60), the *Book of Kells* (MS 58) and the *Garland of Howth* (MS 56).

Fig 2.
The Long Room of the
Old Library, Trinity College
Dublin

The manuscripts came into Trinity Library in different ways, as gifts, deposited for safe keeping or as purchases. Together with drawing thousands of visitors every year, as part of a University collection they continue to be the subject of research, and through careful scrutiny, their pages reveal not just the words of the New Testament, but also much about their rich and varied histories.

Fig 3.
Detail. Book of Kells,
fol. 7v

uinum

Cruc

uestame

supene

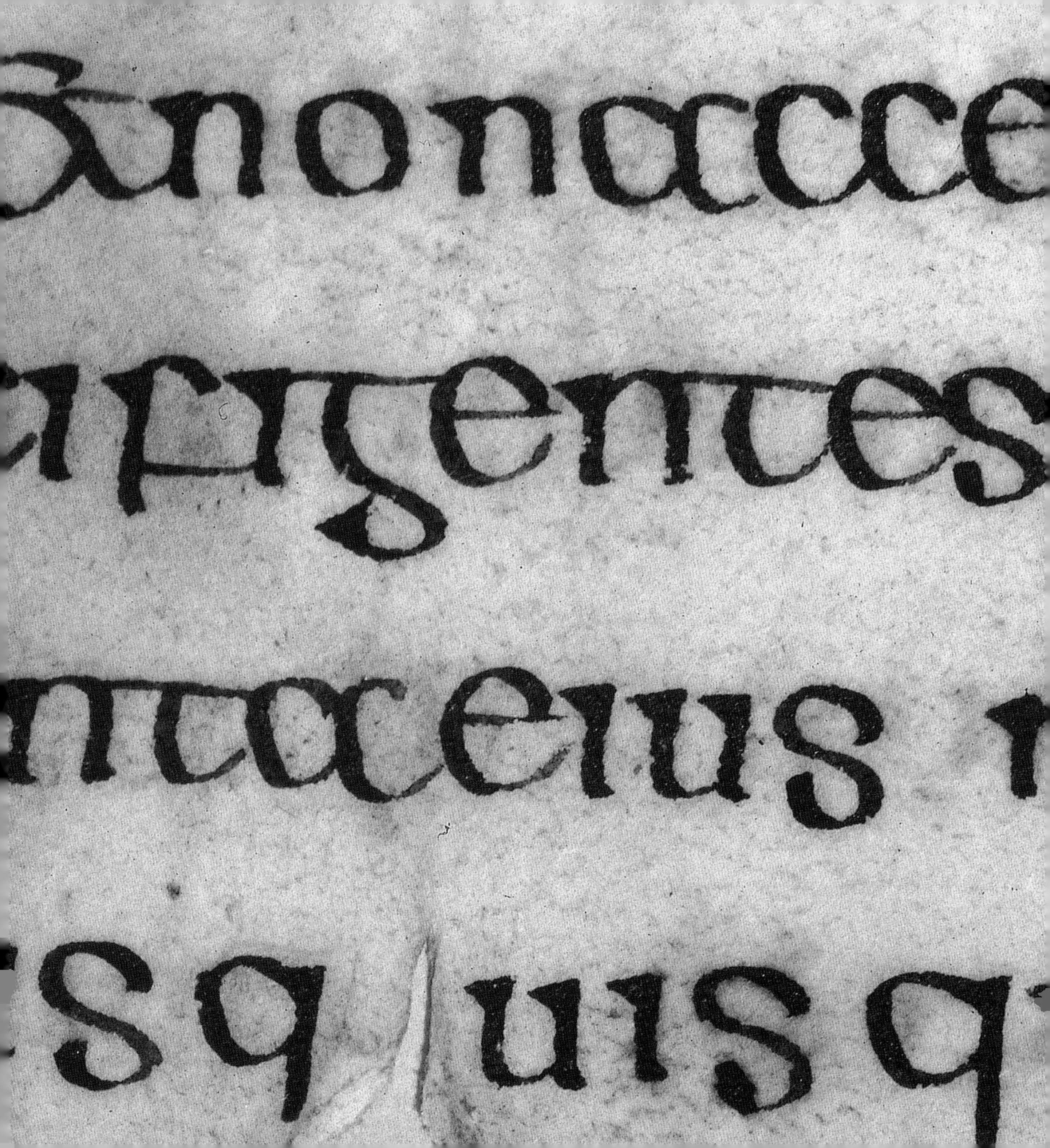
tnonacce
argentes
ntaceius n
sq uisq

How were the gospel books made?

Fig 4.
A late medieval parchment maker stretching and scraping. Stadtbibliothek Nürnberg Amb. 317.2°, fol. 34v. c. 1425

Today we take the manufacture of books for granted, but compiling a manuscript in the early medieval period was far from an easy task. In Ireland the most common writing surface for manuscripts was vellum (from *vitulus*, the Latin word for calf), also known as parchment. Preparation was lengthy, first requiring the skin of a young animal to be soaked in water for several days to begin the rotting process that would loosen the hairs. Lime, vegetable waste or excrement could also be added to speed up the process. The skins were then scraped to remove hairs and loose fatty layers, and stretched on a frame to dry. Re-wetting and scraping on both sides of the skin might be repeated several times before the surface was finished by rubbing it smooth with a pumice stone. By the end of these processes the fibres of the skin had become more uniformly orientated and compact, creating a durable and receptive surface for writing and painting.

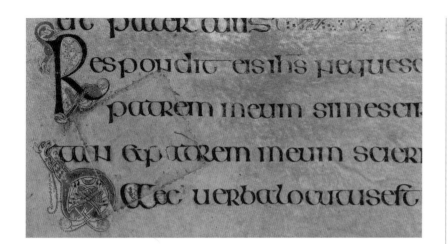

Fig 5.
A patch was stitched onto fol. 316 of the *Book of Kells* to hide an imperfection in the vellum

Cattle were a significant commodity in the cashless society of the time. The value of vellum meant that it was used even when it was of uneven quality, or contained flaws. For example, the vellum used in the *Book of Kells*, taken from an estimated 159 animals, ranges significantly in colour and thickness. Even vellum that had imperfections and holes caused by parasites while the animals were still alive was either patched, or simply incorporated into the overall layout of the page.

Fig 6.
Typically scribes simply wrote around imperfections in the vellum. The scribe of the *Book of Durrow* has actually highlighted a flaw on fol. 121r by outlining it in red ink

The manuscripts are mostly made up of a collection of bifolia, two pages created by folding the parchment in half. In large manuscripts the fold was usually made parallel to, or along the spine of the skin. Several bifolia were placed one inside the other to create a 'quire' which was then sewn together down the centre fold.

Fig 7.
The spine of the calf is visible running vertically down the centre of fol. 28r of *Book of Kells*. The portrait of St Matthew on the verso of the page clearly shows through

Fig 8.
Bifolia of parchment used
to make a quire or single
gathering in a bound book

These were then bound, either into wooden boards equipped with fastenings, or into a soft leather or vellum cover with a fore edge flap, known as a limp binding.

Fig 9.
The original oak binding
boards of the _Book of Armagh_
(shown here on inner and
outer sides) survive, covered
with red goatskin

Fig 10.

A limp binding can be seen in the image of St John from the *Book of Dimma* (p. 104), where the claws of the eagle rest on a book with a scalloped book flap

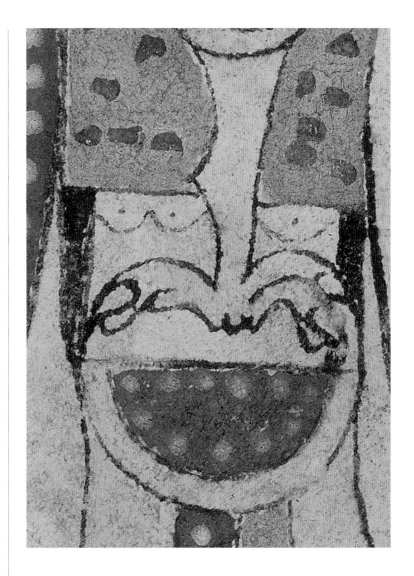

potestas :

Generatio mala et adultera

quaerit et signum non

nisi signum ionae profetae

illis dabitur Et cumuenis

pul eius trans fretum ob

panes accipere :

Qui dixit eis adtendite ·

uos a fermento pharis

Layout and pigments

Fig 11.

The line endings of fol. 76v of the *Book of Kells* are clearly marked with a series of prick marks

As manuscripts were typically bound only after writing and illumination was complete, the scribe needed to know the exact sequence of the text when working on each side of the parchment. Full page illuminations are sometimes on a single folio with a small extension to the edge which could be wrapped around the quire and held by the stitching. While this made life easier for the scribe, ultimately the pages were less secure, leading to losses over the centuries.

Before writing commenced, the page was typically ruled to provide a guide for the scribe. This was done by marking out a series of pricks along inner and outer margins and then scoring the page with a stylus.

Fig 12.

Ruled lines were used in the *Book of Mulling* fol. 73v to establish the layout of the two columns of text

Pages with more complex designs were planned using compasses, templates and possibly even inked stamps for repetitive design features.

29

Inks and pigments were held in containers such as that shown by the side of St Matthew in the *Book of Mulling*, and applied using pens made from hardened quills, and fine brushes.

The ink was typically the gallo-tannic ink known as iron gall ink, made by combining ferrous sulphate and the organic acid extracted from crushed oak gall with a gum binder. This has a warm brown to black tone and is very durable when applied to parchment, although it can fade. Carbon black, made from soot deposits was also used, as were coloured inks. The scribes of the *Book of Kells* used purple, green, yellow and red inks for some of the script.

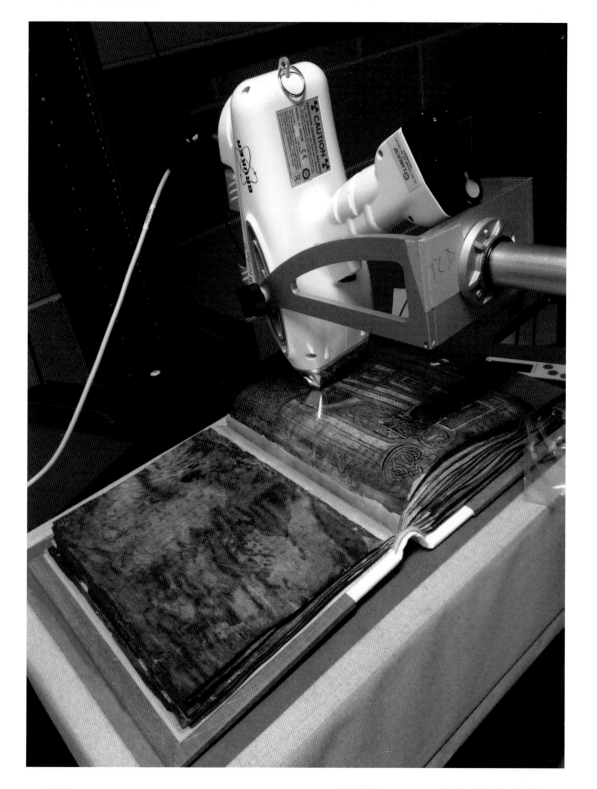

Fig 17.
**The *Garland of Howth*
undergoing non-invasive
analysis using x-ray
fluorescence**

The addition of colour to manuscripts helped to raise their status. As no contemporary Irish pigment recipes survive, non-destructive scientific techniques, including Raman spectroscopy and X-ray fluorescence have been used to ascertain the materials used by some of Ireland's earliest painters.

The earliest manuscripts, such as the *Codex Usserianus Primus* (*c*. 600AD), had a limited palette of iron gall ink and red lead. The bright yellow, used to particularly vibrant effect in the *Book of Durrow* and *Book of Dimma* is from orpiment, a toxic arsenic sulphide also known as *auripigmentum*, or 'gold pigment' due to its use as a substitute for the more expensive material.

Fig 18.
***Codex Usserianus Primus*
fol. 149v. This gospel book
has a very sparing use of
colour and decoration,
limited to black and red**

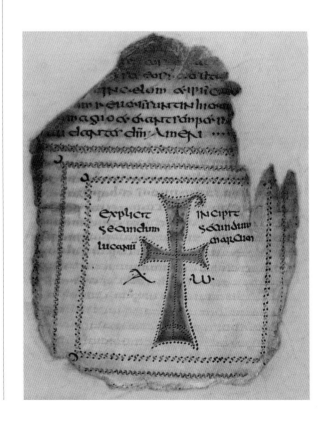

Figs 19 and 20.
Indigo, extracted from the leaves of woad, produced the vibrant blue colour of this cat and fish in the *Book of Kells* fol. 71r

Blue, a colour that also had connotations of high value in the early medieval period, was made from indigo extracted from woad and mixed with white to create a variety of tones. Some greens were made using verdigris, a manufactured copper acetate, which becomes corrosive when moistened. A darker green, known as vergaut, was achieved by mixing orpiment with indigo.

Other pigments, including red and yellow earth pigments, and translucent pinks, oranges, and yellows were also used. These were produced from natural ochres or plant dyes.

Fig 22.
The face of St Mark in the *Book of Mulling* fol. 81v is coloured with chalk white

White was typically made from gypsum or chalk and the purple of the *Book of Kells* has been identified as 'orcein', a dye made from lichen. Binding mediums for pigments have yet to be confirmed, but are likely to have included the white of egg (glair) and the yolk, natural gums and animal gelatine.

All of these pigments could have been procured in Ireland, Britain and continental Europe, and their development and use over a period of at least 500 years suggests a strong continuity of tradition passed from generation to generation.

Fig 23.
An orcein dye produced the purple used to colour this detail on fol. 8r of the *Book of Kells*

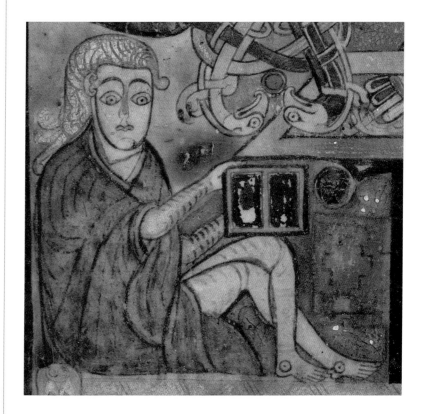

Where were the manuscripts made?

Fig 24.

Fig 24.
Mona Incha, Co. Tipperary.
This small hermitage was
located on an island in
a bog. Tradition held that
St Canice withdrew here
to write a gospel book,
later displayed as a relic
in the church

A number of early accounts of saints' lives refer to holy men and women withdrawing to an isolated spot where they transcribed a gospel book in the spirit of hermetic penance.

For example, in his eighth-century *Life of St Colum Cille*, Abbot Adomnán of Iona made reference to the hut, then still standing on Iona, where the saint had carried out his scribal activity.

Whether these references contain some element of fact, or were simply a means of enhancing the reputation of particular monasteries and the ancient books in their possession is unclear. Certainly by the ninth century there is evidence to suggest that the production of high quality manuscripts was mainly confined to major ecclesiastical foundations, such as Kildare, Clonmacnoise (Co. Offaly), Bangor (Co. Down), Armagh, Clonard (Co. Meath) and Lismore (Co. Waterford).

In 1020 it is recorded that the 'house of the scriptures' *(teach screaptra)* escaped a fire that destroyed much of Armagh, suggesting the presence of a dedicated library or writing room. Unfortunately, no such building remains standing today, but it must have had large windows to facilitate the minute work of the scribes. Archaeological evidence for manuscript production is also scant. At Nendrum, Co. Down, the foundations of a rectangular building (9.14 x 3.96 m) were identified as a possible 'school' due to the discovery of some thin pieces of slate with scratched designs, including neatly executed letter forms, a stylus and a small disc-shaped receptacle, stained red, possibly used for crushing pigment.

Fig 25.
The figure of an ecclesiastic holding a large open book at Lismore, Co. Waterford, one of the foremost seats of learning in early medieval Ireland

Fig 26.
This small piece of slate was probably used by a scribe working at Nendrum to practise letter forms ('b', 'c' and 'e') and designs

HORUM TRIGINTA

ioseo

uı

uı

uı

puto

puı

puı

t ut putabatur fil

h

heli

mattha

leui

Scribes and artists

Ecclesiastical establishments were certainly the principal centres of learning for boys and girls, both lay and religious. An insight into teaching methods is provided in the *Life of St Canice*, the saint who wrote on wax for his student to copy. This is a reference to waxed wooden tablets, like those found in Springmount Bog, Co. Antrim – a cheaper surface than vellum on which to practice. Occasionally the hands of different scribes can also be detected in the text of the manuscripts, which may also attest to teaching practice.

erit relinquetur. due erunt molentes
in unum una assumetur & alt pelinquetur. duo
in agro unus assumetur & alius relinquetur.
Respondentes dixerunt ubi dno qui dixit eis ubi
cumque fuerit corpus illuc congregabuntur
aquile. Dicebat aut & parabulam ad illos quo
oportet semper orare & non deficere dicens in
civitate quedam erat in quadam civitate quidam
iudex qui deum non timebat & hominem non reverebatur. Vidua
autem quedam erat in civitate illa & veniebat ad eum dicens. Vindica me
de adversario meo. Et nolebat per multum tempus. Post
hec autem dixit intra se. Et si deum non timeo nec hominem revereor ta
men quia molesta est mihi hec vidua vindicabo illam ne in novissi
mo veniens sugillet me. Ait autem dominus. Audite quid iudex
iniquitatis dicit. deus autem non faciet vindicta electorum suorum cla
mantium ad se die ac nocte & patientiam habe
bit in illis. dico vobis quia faciet vindictam illo
rum cito. verum tamen filius hominis veniens pu
tas inveniet fidem in terra. Dixit autem & ad quosdam qui
in se confidebant tamquam iusti & spernebant
alios. Duo homines ascenderunt in templum ut
orarent. Unus pharisseus & alter publicanus. Phariseus
stans hec apud se orabat. deus gratias
ago tibi quia non sum sicut ceteri homi
nes raptores iniusti adulteri velut etiam hic

...tendum parte ouium me
si ul sacra me
Rogo beatitudinem
tuam sce pater beatitudo
p(er)quaci utquicuique
hunclibellum in manu te
nuerit meminerit cælum
bas scriptorū qui hoc s(er)m
...iut euuangelium. per...
dierum spatium... ...anum

Fig 29.
Detail of the (altered)
colophon on fol. 247v of the
Book of Durrow, which in
translation from the Latin
reads 'I ask your beatitude
presbyter Patrick, that
whoever holds in his
hand this little book may
remember [me] Columba
the writer who wrote this
Gospel for myself in the
space of twelve days by
 the grace of our Lord s.s.'

Maél Brigte, a scribe working in Armagh in the early twelfth century, recorded that he had completed his gospel book (BL MS Harl. 1802) at the age of twenty-eight. The minute scale that characterises the ornamentation of these books, executed before the known introduction of magnifying lenses, together with the toxicity of many of the pigments used, suggests that scribes, like him, would have been relatively young.

Depending on the scale and complexity of the text, some manuscripts were completed by an individual, while others were collaborative efforts. It is estimated that at least seven scribes and artists were involved in the making of the *Book of Kells,* while other books were both written and illustrated by a single hand. An inscription, or colophon, in the *Book of Durrow* asks for readers to remember Columba, the scribe who wrote the book for himself in twelve days. However, given the carefully executed script and complex illumination of the manuscript, one modern calligrapher has suggested that about eight months would be required for a single scribe to complete the work, so the inscription may allude to an earlier model from which the text was copied, rather than the *Book of Durrow* itself.

Different books
and their development

Fig 30.

Canon table in the *Book of Kells* (fol. 5r) facilitating the cross-referencing of passages in the New Testament across the four gospels

Although sharing many common attributes, Irish gospel books differed considerably in content, size, type of script and decoration according to their intended final use.

By the third century AD a piecemeal accumulation of Latin translations of the gospel texts was in circulation, known collectively as the *vestusa translatio* or 'Old Latin Bible'. Trinity's oldest gospel book, the *Codex Usserianus Primus* contains a text of this type. In 382, Pope Damasus I commissioned St Jerome to devise a new translation, based on the older translations and original Greek and Hebrew texts. This became known as the *editio vulgata* or the vulgate. Although the vulgate eventually became the standard text used by the Western Church, its full adoption was not immediate, and mixed 'Old Latin' and vulgate readings are a feature of most early Irish gospel texts.

Together with the four gospel texts, both Old Latin and vulgate gospel books often contained additional introductory material. This included brief synopses of the contents of each gospel known either as *capitulae* (little chapters) or *breves causae* (brief topics) and the etymologies of Hebrew names. The vulgate also included the Prefaces of St Jerome, relating to the translation of the gospels and introduction to the canon tables, a system for cross-referencing parallel passages across the gospels.

The *Book of Kells*, justifiably the most famous of the surviving books, originally contained all of these elements. Measuring 33cm x 25.5cm it is large and the scribes made generous use of the vellum. The text is written in a clear, measured form known as majuscule, in a style that was distinctive to the Irish Church. These features, together with the lavish decoration in a relatively wide range of colours indicate that this was a luxury gospel, intended as much for display as for liturgical use. Records of other, now lost, display gospels at important Irish monasteries suggest that it may not have been unique. For example, a 'great gospel of St Matthew' (*Matha Mór*), associated with St Ciaran, was displayed on his altar with other relics at Clonmacnoise in the eleventh century, and the 'Great gospel of Kildare' was described with awe by the twelfth-century commentator, Gerald of Wales.

Fig 31.
A fascimile of the *Book of Kells* showing its large size

Fig 32.
Majuscule script in the *Book of Kells* fol. 35v. This is characterised by 'upper and lower case' letters, usually of even height

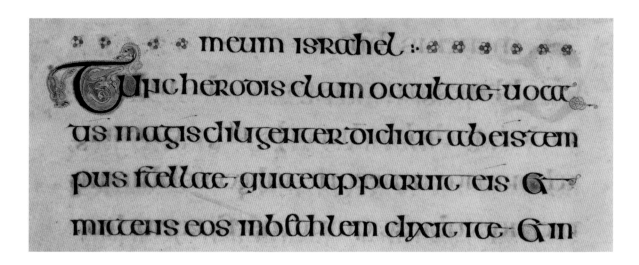

1

[Latin manuscript, Insular minuscule, heavily abbreviated — New Testament text, end of First Epistle and beginning of Second Epistle to the Corinthians]

... explicit prima ad chorinthios ...

... incipit ... ad chorinthios ...

Paulus apostolus ...
... grata uobis & pax a deo
patre nostro & domino iesu christo ...
Benedictus deus & pater domini nostri iesu christi
misericordiarum & deus totius consolationis
qui consolatur nos in omni tribulatione
ut possimus & ipsi consolari eos qui
in omni angustia per consolationem qua
consolamur & ipsi a deo quoniam & habund...
... passiones christi in nobis ita per christum
habundat etiam consolatio nostra sive tri-
bulamur pro uestra consolatione & salute sive op...
... consolamini eandem quam passionum quas &
nos patimur ut spes nostra firma sit pro uobis
... hortamur pro uestra consolatione & salute
... & quis passionum quae per poenitentiam
... consolationis ...

Nolumus enim uos ignorare fratres de tribula-
tione nostra ... quae facta est ... in asia quoniam supra
modum grauati sumus supra uirtutem
... ut taederet nos etiam uiuere sed ipsi in nobis ipsis
... habuimus ut non ... simus fidentes
in nobis sed in deo qui suscitat mortuos
... de tantis periculis eripuit nos & eruet in quem ...
... quoniam & adhuc eripiet adiuuantibus & uobis
in oratione pro nobis ut ex multorum facie ...
... donationis per multos gratiae
... pro nobis gloria est nostra testi-
monium conscientiae nostrae quoniam in simpli-
citate & sinceritate dei & non in sapientia car-
nali sed in gratia dei conuersati sumus in hoc mundo
habundantius ... ad uos ...

Fig 33.
The *Book of Armagh*,
fol. 122r, opening
to Corinthians II

Possession of such a manuscript helped to elevate the status of the monastery in which it was kept. The *Book of Armagh*, uniquely, contains a complete copy of the New Testament, together with transcriptions of writings of St Patrick and extracts from the *Life of St Martin of Tours*, one of the founding fathers of monasticism. The combination of these texts was quite deliberate, and was a means for the book's patron, Abbot Torbach (d. 807AD), to strengthen Armagh's bid for ecclesiastical supremacy in Ireland through promoting (and exaggerating) its unique relationship with the national saint. Within just over a century of its creation, the book had become an emblem of the office of abbot of Armagh, one of the most senior ecclesiastical posts in the land.

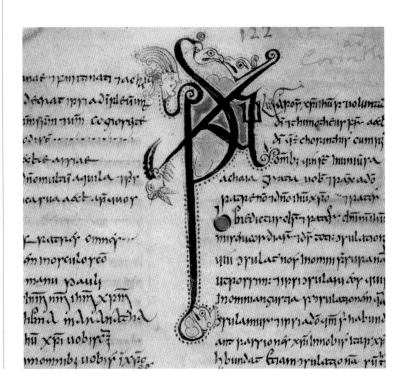

In contrast, both the *Book of Dimma* and *Book of Mulling* were most likely made for personal use. Described by modern scholars as 'pocket gospels' these tiny books, measuring 17.5cm x 14.2 cm and 16.5 x 12cm respectively, contain or contained the text of the four gospels written in a speedily executed cursive form of handwriting termed insular minuscule, with numerous abbreviations. Though now both incomplete, it seems that illustrations were limited to the openings of the gospels, and while the *Book of Mulling* now contains some introductory material, originally both omitted this.

Fig 34.
The *Book of Mulling*. Small enough to fit comfortably in the hand

Fig 35.
Minuscule script on fol. 27r of the *Book of Mulling*. This is characterised by 'lower case' letters where the ascenders and descenders of letter forms extend beyond the body of the letter

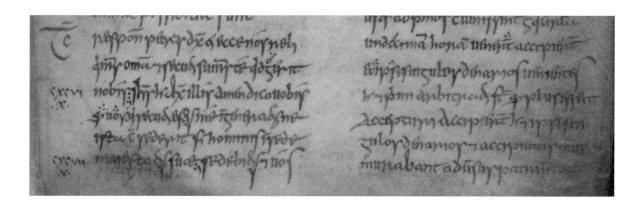

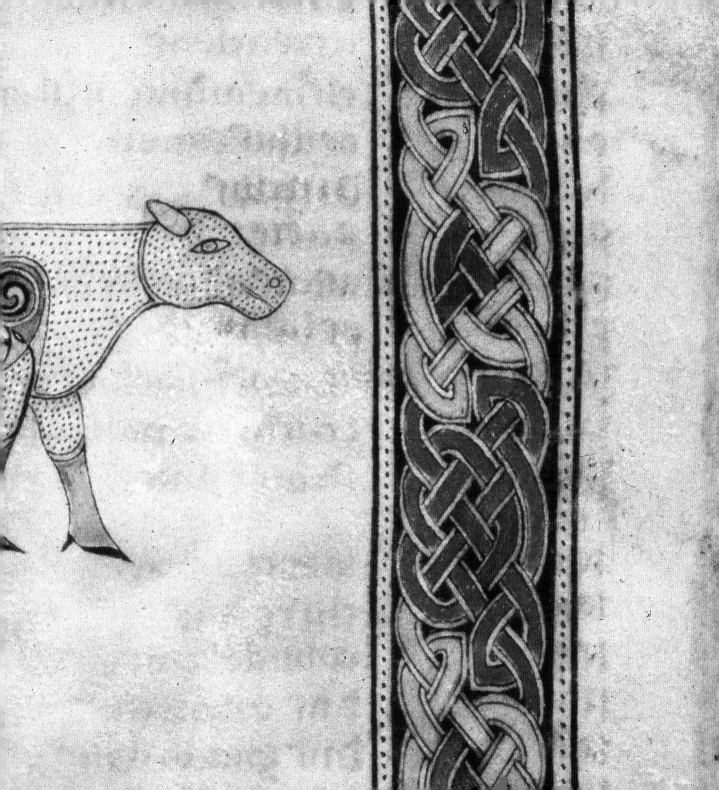

Fig 37.

The opening of the gospel of St Mark in the *Garland of Howth* (fol.22r) shows the evangelist holding his book, with his symbol, the lion, above and the opening words of his gospel *Initium eua[ngelli]*

Fig 36.

The sequence of pages that mark the opening of the gospel of St Luke in the *Book of Durrow* (fols 124v-126r) starts with the evangelist depicted as his symbol, the calf and a blank folio on one opening, followed by an opening with a page of pure decoration and the enlarged letters of the opening of his gospels *Quoniam*

The ornamentation

More than anything, it is the decoration of early Irish gospel books that sets them apart from contemporary manuscripts created elsewhere. Although no two manuscripts are the same, there is a general pattern in the sections that were singled out for particular decoration. In larger books these were usually the canon-table pages; then, preceding each gospel, a 'portrait' of the evangelist and/ or his symbol (man, lion, calf or eagle), a full page of elaborately patterned ornament known as a 'carpet page' facing the enlarged, richly decorated letters that marked the opening or incipit of each gospel text. The opening of St Mark's Gospel in the *Garland of Howth* combines the 'portrait', decoration and opening of the text on a single page. Important sections of text might also be highlighted with enlarged letters or the addition of ornament.

Additional decorated pages are found in some texts. These include illustrations of the four evangelists in their symbolic form positioned around a cross, as for example in the *Book of Armagh* – a visual expression of the harmony between the accounts written by the evangelists in their gospels. Scenes from the Life and Passion of Christ are more unusual, and typically highly stylized. *The Book of Kells* includes depictions of the enthroned Virgin and Child with Angels (fol. 7v), an enigmatic image probably alluding to different episodes from the Passion of Christ (fol. 144v) and Temptation of Christ (fol. 202v).

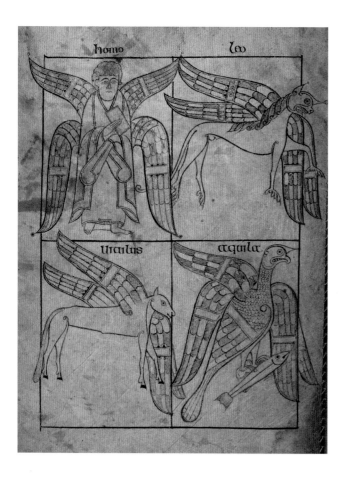

Fig 39.
Book of Kells fol. 7v contains one of the earliest depictions of the Virgin and Child in a western manuscript and probably takes its influence from a Byzantine icon

Fig 38.
The four evangelists, Matthew the man, Mark the lion, Luke the calf and John the eagle in the *Book of Armagh* fol. 32v

The *Book of Kells* is also distinguished from the other manuscripts in the collection by the sheer number and quality of illustrations added to the minor initials and between the lines of the text. Cats, birds, lizards, hares and goats together with warriors and horsemen enliven the pages in a colourful and often playful manner that is sometimes difficult to reconcile with the sacred nature of the text.

Fig 40.
The stripy cat on fol 48r of the *Book of Kells* is shown with a rat as it escapes with the communion host

Fig 41.
A lizard scuttles across the lines of text on fol. 72r

Fig 42.
This figure, entwined with lions and birds, marks the beginning of Christ's genealogy in the gospel of St Luke on fol. 200r of the *Book of Kells*.

Fig 43.
An exhibitionist warrior shown crouching at the bottom of fol. 200r of the *Book of Kells* has his foot ensnared in the letter 'h'

Fig 44.
The greyhound and hare on fol. 48r of the *Book of Kells* are placed beneath the text that reads 'how much more will your father who is in heaven give good things to them that ask him?'

In pocket gospels the more sparing ornament was limited to an evangelist portrait and enlarged initial to mark the start of each gospel. A curious diagram at the end of the *Book of Mulling* (fol. 94v) was once thought to represent the monastic enclosure at St Mullin's, Co. Carlow, but is now believed to be a visual prompt for the prayers that accompany it.

Fig 45.

A portrait of St Luke holding his gospel faces the start of his text in the *Book of Dimma* pp. 54-55

Fig 46.

A copy of the diagram from the *Book of Mulling*

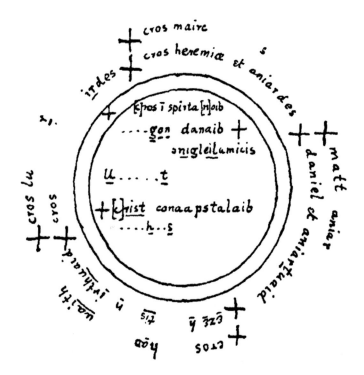

Figs 47, 48.
Detail of spirals and whorls from a carpet page in the *Book of Durrow* (fol. 3v) and XPI monograph of Christ's name in the gospel of St Matthew from the *Book of Armagh* (fol. 33v)

The designation of 'Celtic' often given to these manuscripts arises from their inclusion of ornamentation fashioned from tightly sprung spirals and whorls. These trace their ancestry to the art current in Ireland prior to the arrival of Christianity, and it remains a puzzle as to why this essentially pagan art form was seen as appropriate to decorate the most holy of objects.

Fig 49.
Pre-Christian Romano-Celtic brooch with spiral designs *c.* AD 200

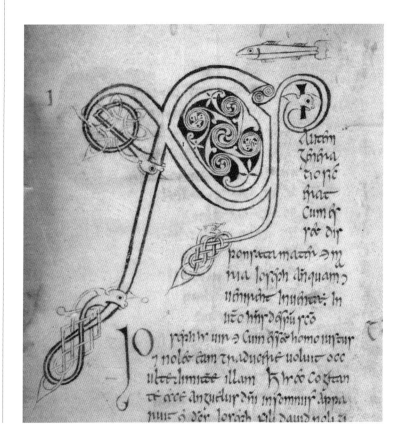

In addition, many pages are inhabited by a menagerie of contorted or interlaced animals. These are ultimately derived from the art of the non-Christian Germanic peoples, although some have argued that Christian interpretations can be applied to the particular genuses depicted, such as lions, peacocks and snakes.

Fig 50.
Detail from fol. 192v of the _Book of Durrow_, showing abstracted, interlaced quadrupeds

Fig 51.
Detail of fol. 34r of the _Book of Kells_. Each panel of ornament includes a beautifully balanced design of interlaced humans, lions, snakes and birds

um & milita...

or & att il...

...alump nicum...

...peidit dii...

d·cogta...

The extended lives of the manuscripts

Fig 52.
Codex Usserainus Primus
**fol. 86r between some of
the lines an Irish scribe has
scratched in Old Irish the
word *fochr(a)ic* meaning
wages or payments**

Trinity College Dublin's early Irish gospel books range in age from about 1,100 – 1,400 years old and the story of their survival is as important as that of their making.

Close study can sometimes reveal how they were used over time. Several pages of the *Codex Usserianus Primus* incorporate glosses – notes on the text – scratched into the page using a metal stylus. These are barely visible to the naked eye (the page must be turned to the raking light to see them), perhaps so as not to distract subsequent readers. As some are written in Old Irish, they are a good indication that this Latin gospel text was being studied by an Irish person at an early time.

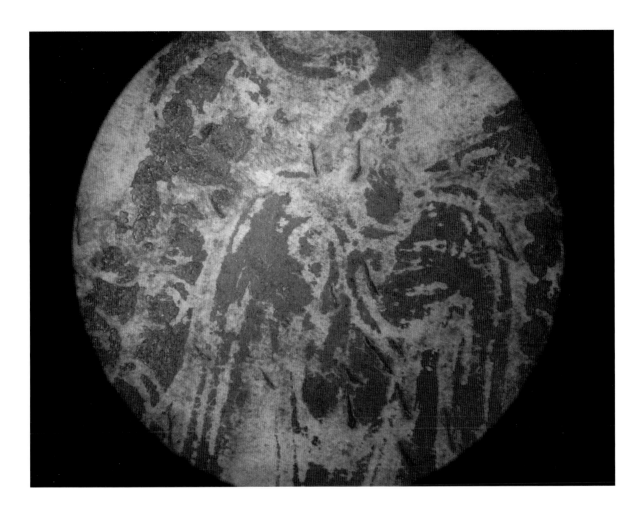

Figs 53 and 54.
Book of Kells, **fol. 202v,**
detail showing the devil
and the stab marks to
his chest

When observed under a microscope, the figure of the Devil on fol 202v of the *Book of Kells* revealed a more sinister secret. He had been stabbed multiple times, possibly not long after the book's creation.

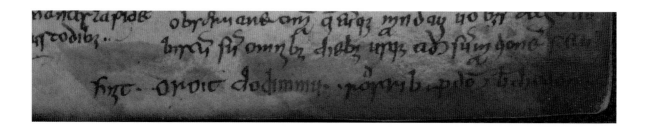

Perhaps by virtue of their very survival during turbulent times, by the mid-tenth century there is evidence to suggest that many of these books had come to be regarded as holy relics. The *Book of Mulling* incorporates an inscription attributing its writing to 'Moling', which ultimately led to the belief that it had been written by St Moling himself. Where such saintly attributions did not exist, some 'constructive alteration' might take place. In the *Book of Dimma* for example, the original scribe, Danchairde's name was carefully removed in three of its four occurrences and replaced with the name Dimma. Dimma was, according to tradition, the scribe of St Crónán of Roscrea, who had managed to write an entire gospel book in 'one' day, thanks to the miraculous intervention of the saint in preventing the sun from setting for 40 nights. The careful erasure of the names of the *Book of Armagh* scribes probably had a similar motivation, the desire to distance the book's authorship from association with earthly hands.

The sacred nature of these objects led to their use in a number of unexpected ways. The pages of both the *Book of Kells* and *Book of Armagh* provided an enduring space for the recording of legal agreements, carrying the additional attraction of being 'sealed' on a holy relic. Legal agreements noted in the *Book of Armagh*, and the *Book of Kells*, dated to the eleventh and twelfth centuries, mainly relate to local land deals.

Fig 55.
At the end of the gospel of St Matthew in the *Book of Dimma* p. 29 is the inscription (translated from Irish) '*Finit*. A prayer for Dimma who wrote [this] for God; and a benediction'. The 'Dimma' is a later addition over an erased name

Fig 56.
A text inserted around the year 1005 into the *Book of Armagh* fol. 16v (bottom right) celebrates king Brian Boru as *Imperator Scotorum* (Emperor of the Irish). It was written to record an agreement between Brian and Ireland's most powerful church, Armagh

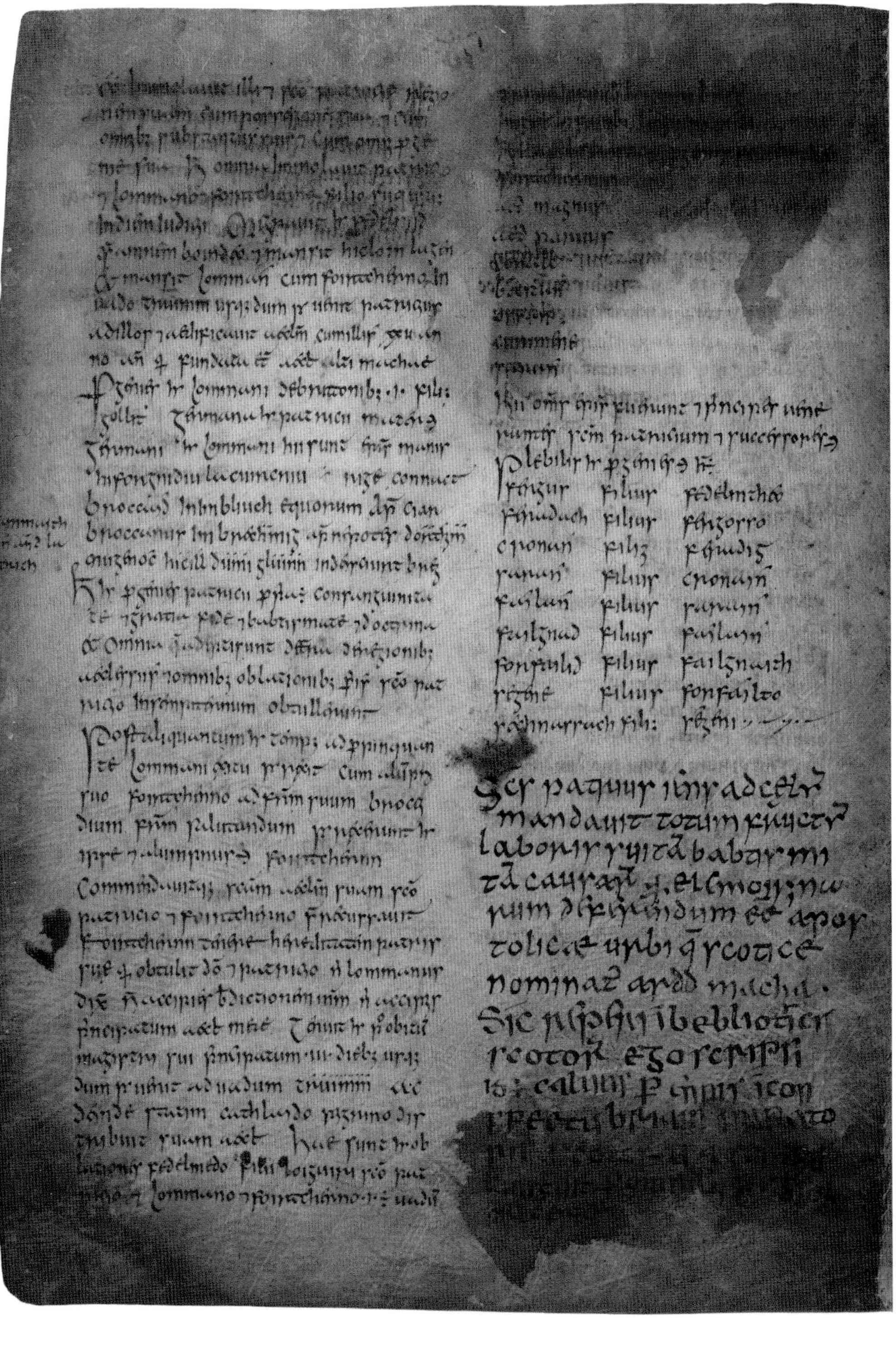

Left column

Cú brunel auit illi ⁊ feo peccatis plebio
a ḟothnuidn cum porczhanu... euan ⁊ ...
omnib; ṗ ubraeniar emer Cum omni ṗ...
me fuu. H omnu humolum peccatis
⁊ ḟommuno... diazba filio ṁug ḃru...
indiem iudicii. Oiḟcaruu... ḃ ...ḟtu uṡ
ḟ omnum bennded ⁊ manrie hiclo in luzin
la manzie ḟomman cum ḟontchina in
uido triumm uṗ; dum ṗ uinie patruciuṡ
adilloṗ ⁊ acḣṗicauu acclḣn camilli geu an
no un ḟ fundatu ẜ acct alzi machue
Pzoiuḣ ḣ ḟomnani deḃruconib; ·t· filu
ḟolli Zomanu ḣ pacmen muchig
Zoimani ḣ ḟomnani hu funt ḣuṡ manu
ṁ fonzmdiu lucunenu · nige connuce
hnoccaib Inbnbluch equonum aṗ cian
hnoccunur Im bṗecḣimz aṗ nṗocḣ dozchin
onzṁoe hieill dunu gliunn indoraunt buḣ
H ḣ pzoiuḣ pacmen pṡuṡ conṗunzunnia
ze ⁊znacio ṗẜe ⁊ buḃurmaze ⁊ doczina
ẜ omniu ḥadnicirunt ẜffnu ḋnicionib;
acclẜnuṡ nomnib; oblacionib; ḣiṡ ṗẜo pat
nicio ṁ ṗonṁnamum obzullaunu—
Poṡz ali quancum ḣ comṗ; adṗpinguen
ze ḟommani adcu pṗ geẜ cum alṗ pu
nuo ḟontchino adṗim nuum hnocc
dium pṡun ṗilicundum pṗ geẜunu ḣ
ipṗe ⁊ alumpnuṡ ḟontchoinu
Commḃdunuzg; nuim acclu nuum ṗẜo
pacnicio ⁊ ḟontchino ḟ nacurṗauu
ḟontchoinu zoiche· hṗe llacion pacnu
nuṡ ḟ obzuliz dẜ ⁊ pacnicio ṁ ḟommanuṡ
diẜ H accipuṡ ḃdicionon nuin ḟ accipuṡ
pnciṗazum acct ṁ̄ne· Zoinuṡ ḣ ṗṡobuzi
machṗin ṡuu pnciṗazum ·iii· diebuṡ uṗg;
dum pṡunuṡ adnuadum triumu · ace
donde pacim cachlendo ṗgzuno diṗ
znubuz nuam acct· Hae ṡunt noḃ
lacionuṡ pedelmedo filii zoiguṗu ṗẜo pat
nicio ⁊ ḟommano ⁊ ṗontchoino ·i·ẜ nadiṡ

(left margin): ṁṁuzch aṗ uiẜ lu ...zuch

Right column

...
...
...
acct magnuṡ   ... acct ṁ̄ ...
acct pamuṡ
ḟ...ẜe nuzlazul ...
aẜ...cilẜ ṗdiuṡ
aṗ ṗiṡ
cummñe
ṗ auni

Hu omṗ cuṗ pucdune ⁊ pncipuṡ uine
puncuṗ ṗẜm pacnciuṁ ⁊ ṗuceẜ ṗopfẜ
Plebilr ḣ pẜ mḣ ⁊ ẜ

	filiur	
Fergur	filiur	Fedelmtheo
Finnduach	filiur	Fhzorro
Cronan	fili	Fhiudig
Ranain	filiur	Cronain
Faelan	filiur	Ranain
Failgnad	filiur	Failini
Fonfalad	filiur	Failgnaich
Regme	filiur	Fonfailteo
Rechnarrach	fili	Regmi —

Ger paquuṗ iuṁ adcellu
mandauut zozum euuceṗ
labonuṗ ṗuicd babor m
zu cauṗagu ⁊ elċmoṁ nuṁ
nuum dlẜ ṗicḣdum ẜẜ aṗoṡ
zolice uṗbu ⁊ ṗcozice
nominaz aṗdd machu ·
Sic nṡṗṡu i beḃliozḣc
ṗcozoṗ ego ṗcnṗṡi
ib; cailuṗ Ṗ cinuṗ icon
ṗfẜ dicub; nuṗ niṁ uzo
...

Elevation to the status of relic led the books ultimately to be enshrined in jewel encrusted cases or covers. Although the function of the shrine was to protect and elevate the status of the relic within, the shrine that housed the *Codex Usserianus Primus* evidently had a high copper content and caused serious damage, corroding all of the outer edges of the folios.

The *Book of Durrow* was given such a case in the very early tenth century by king Flann Sinna mac Máel Sechnaill, with a request for St Columba's blessing on the king engraved around a silver cross on the cover, and in 937, Flann's son Donnchad provided a similar shrine for the *Book of Armagh*. These, like the jewelled cover of the *Book of Kells*, stolen in 1007, are now lost, but the shrines of the *Book of Dimma* and *Book of Mulling* still survive.

Fig 57.
Codex Usserianus Primus **showing damage to the edges of the manuscript caused by its shrine**

Fig 58.
Shrine of the *Book of Dimma*. The inscription around the rim records that it was gilded by Thaddeus O Carroll, 'King of Eile' [1380-1407] and restored by Domnaldus O Cuanain [a cleric]. The name of the goldsmith was Tomás

Inscriptions on these shrines suggest that by the late fourteenth century, the books were as much royal insignia as they were holy relics, and that association with or possession of them helped to elevate the status and territorial claims of the O'Carroll and Kavanagh families respectively. Gospel books were also sometimes used by secular potentates as battle talismans such as the gospel book of St Finbar of Cork, used by Munster king Mathgamain mac Cinneidigh in 976 when he went into battle.

Fig 59.
Inscription on the *Book of Mulling* shrine naming Arthur [mac Murrough Kavanagh] 'King of Leinster' in 1402

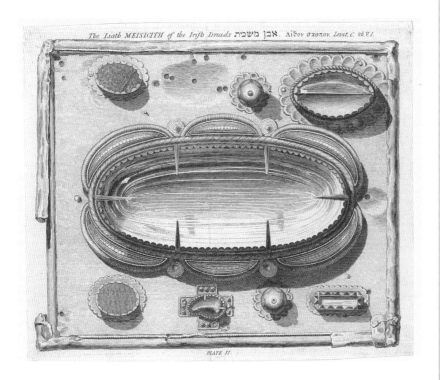

The Liath MEISICITH of the Irish Druids אבן משבית. Λίθον σκοπον. Levit. c. 26.V.I.

PLATE II.

artturus
rex domin
us 3 lagenie
elnsdabe
tilia 3 baroni
anno 3 dni
millio
quadrin
gentesi
mo scdo
aD

84

Fig 60.
Ireland's Eye Island located off the coast of Howth, Co. Dublin, with Puck's or Devil's Rock in the foreground

According to tradition, the *Garland of Howth* was used by St Nessan to expel a devil from his island monastery of Ireland's Eye, near Dublin. The devil was propelled into the adjacent cliff-face with such force that it cleft the rock, a feature that retains the name 'Puck's' or 'Devil's' Rock. By the sixteenth century the people of nearby Howth were afraid to swear oaths on the *Garland*, due to the terrible fate that might befall them if they broke their word.

Books were also used for cures. This function probably explains the later addition of prayers for the visitation of the sick to the pages of both the *Book of Dimma* and the *Book of Mulling*. The curative properties of the *Book of Durrow* were released in a more physical way. In 1627, it was noted that the custodian of the book used it as a remedy when his cattle were sick, by immersing it in their water. Miraculously the cattle returned to 'their former pristine state', while the book was said to have remained unharmed. In fact, the water reacted with the copper acetate of the green pigment, causing serious damage to the vellum.

Fig 61.
Garland of Howth **fol. 1r showing the wear and tear of use over the centuries**

Fig 62.
Book of Durrow, fol 1v
showing damage caused
to the opening page of the
gospel in areas coloured
with verdigris

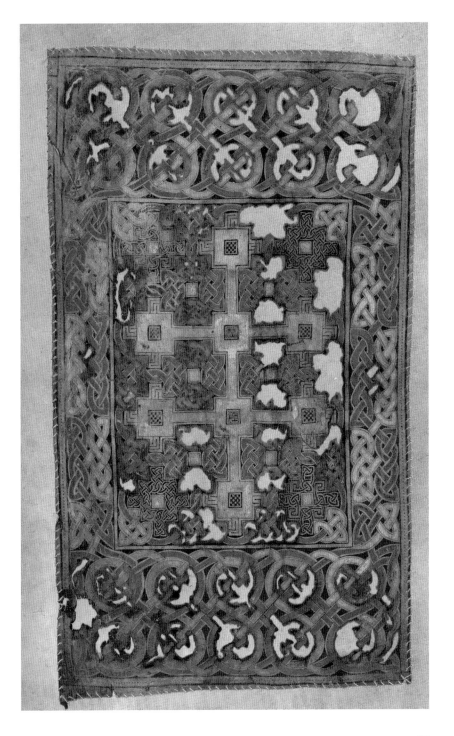

The manuscripts and the future

Fig 63.
Micro-Raman
spectroscopic analysis
of the *Book of Mulling*
to determine the nature
of the pigments used

Although there is now a better understanding of the manuscripts, and the appropriate way to care for them, many questions remain unanswered.

We will probably never know the names of the artists, or the exact circumstances that led to the creation of such masterpieces as the *Book of Kells*. However, careful scrutiny of the texts and images of the manuscripts continue to reveal clues as to the models that the scribes may have used and the cultures from which they drew their inspiration. Further scientific research and analysis also has the potential to reveal more about the artists' methods, the exact nature of the pigments that they used and ultimately, perhaps, the sources of their vellum. When placed in the context of similar research internationally, this will provide a clearer insight into the training of Irish craftsmen, how their skills developed over time, and perhaps even the geographical locations where they worked.

Since their creation, gospel books have been available only to a very limited audience, whether as personal possessions carried and used by individuals, as lavishly decorated gospels displayed on an altar of a special chapel, as relics entirely removed from view in sealed shrines, or museum artefacts with single openings placed on view in a glass case.

Thanks to digital technology this has now changed, and many of the manuscripts are now available to a global audience.

In 1185, the cleric Gerald of Wales encountered the great gospel book of Kildare and exclaimed that

> 'if you take the trouble to look very closely, and penetrate with your eyes the secrets of the artistry, you will notice such intricacies, so delicate and subtle, so close together and well-knitted, so involved and bound together, and so fresh still in their colourings that you will not hesitate to declare that all these things must have been the result of the work, not of men, but of angels'.

Just under 1,000 years after these lines were written, modern viewers may now follow Gerald's advice, by exploring in minute detail the artistry of Trinity's early medieval manuscripts at http://digitalcollections.tcd.ie/home/

Fig 64.
The digital *Book of Dimma*

Further Reading

Henderson, George,
*From Durrow to Kells, the
Insular Gospel-books 650–800*
(London, 1987)

Henry, Françoise,
*Irish Art during the Early
Christian Period to 800*
(London, 1965)

Henry, Françoise,
*Irish Art during the Viking
Invasions: 800–1020 A.D.*
(London 1967)

Meehan, Bernard,
The Book of Kells
(London, 2012)

Meehan, Bernard,
*The Book of Durrow:
A Medieval Masterpiece
at Trinity College Dublin*
(Dublin, 1996)

Meehan, Bernard,
'"A Melody of Curves across the
Page": Art and Calligraphy in
the Book of Armagh', *Irish Arts
Review* 14 (1998), pp. 90–101

Moss, Rachel, *Art and
Architecture of Ireland.
Volume 1. Medieval
c. 400-1600AD* (London,
New Haven and Dublin, 2014)

O'Neill, Timothy,
*The Irish Hand. Scribes and
their Manuscripts from the
Earliest Times* (Cork, 2014)

Pulliam, Heather,
*Word and Image in the
Book of Kells* (Dublin, 2006)

Glossary

Anglo-Saxon the term used to describe the culture current in Britain c. 500-1066 during which it was largely ruled by the Germanic Angles and Saxons

Bifolium (pl. bifolia) a piece of parchment or paper folded in half to produce two leaves (i.e. four pages)

Binding the stitching together and covering of a book

Byzantine term used to refer to the culture focussed around the ancient city of Byzantium (now Istanbul), which fused Greek, Roman and Christian elements.

Canon table A system whereby numbers placed in the margins of the gospel texts correspond to a table that indicates concordance of passages between the different gospels.

Carpet page An ornamental page, particularly favoured in Insular art, typically used to preface each gospel text

Celtic A term used to refer to an Iron Age culture current across Europe in the pre-Christian era, but which lingered along the north Atlantic into the early Christian period

Chi Rho A monogram composed of the letter XP (the Greek Chi and Rho), the first two characters of Christ's name. In Insular gospel books the start of Matthew 1:18 typically has an elaborately embellished Chi Rho

Codex a book composed of folded sheets sewn along one edge

Codicology the study of the physical structure of a book

Colophon an inscription recording information relating to the production of a book

Display script decorated script, usually of a higher grade than the adjacent text, often used to emphasise the opening of a particular passage

Evangelist portraits depictions of the authors of the four gospels typically placed at the start of their respective gospels

Evangelist symbols Symbols derived from Ezekiel's vision of four heavenly creatures: the man, lion, ox and eagle (Ezekiel 1:1-14), conflated with the four 'living creatures' that surround God's throne, as described in *Revelation* 4:7. Early Christian writers linked different evangelists with different creatures. In Irish art two interpretations are found: that of St Irenaeus of Lyons (Matthew-man, John-lion, Luke-ox and Mark-eagle), for example in the Book of Durrow , and, more commonly, that of St Jerome (Matthew-man, Mark-lion, Luke-ox and John-eagle).

Exemplar a book from which another is copied

Folio a sheet of writing material

Gospel book the text of the four accounts of Christ's life attributed to Matthew, Mark, Luke and John

Icon a venerated likeness of a sacred person or subject

Iconography the subject or meaning of an image

Incipit the opening words of a text (from the Latin *incipere*)

Insular Deriving from the Latin *insula* (island), the term is used to describe the artistic style current in Ireland and areas under Irish cultural influence from *c*. 600–*c*. 900, elements of which persisted until the sixteenth century

Interlace decoration consisting of apparently interwoven strands

Limp binding a binding made of parchment, soft leather or fabric without boards

Majuscule large letters, often in upper case, in which all the letters are the same height

Manuscript a book written by hand, abbreviated in the singular to ms, plural mss

Minuscule small letters written cursively and in lower case

Parchment a writing support made from prepared animal hide. The term vellum is typically reserved for calf skin

Pigment the colouring agent in paint

Pricking the marking of a folio with a sharp point to guide the layout of a page.

Quire the gatherings of bifolia from which a book is formed

Raman spectroscopy a non-destructive technique by which the molecules present in material may be identified

Recto the front side of a folio, abbreviated to r

Scriptorium a room used for writing

Stylus a pointed implement used for writing on wax tablets and pricking an ruling manuscripts

Verso the back of a folio, abbreviated as v

X-ray fluorescence spectroscopy a non-destructive method of investigating pigments that provides elemental information about inorganic materials

Graphic Design: Red&Grey
Print: managed by Custodian Consultancy